ALPHA MALE:

COMPLETE GUIDE

How to be an Alpha Male that
Hot Chicks Can't Resist

By Marco Angelo

Published by Media Prestige eBook
Publishing Company

© Copyright 2015

Table of Contents

CHAPTER 1: WHO IS AN ALPHA MALE?

Whatever you know about what it is to be an Alpha, get rid of it. If you want to know the real meaning of being an Alpha, you'll have to drain away all existing knowledge of it first.

In primal nature, to be an Alpha means to be the physically strongest in a group. However, in the world of Man, the Alpha doesn't have to be the strongest nor the smartest. He just has to create the image in everybody's mind that he is. In other words, to be an Alpha in the human world depends on one's ability to project strength or confidence, and project it so greatly that others believe it to be a reality.

In this manner of thinking, you classify yourself based on others' projection of their image into your mind. In simpler terms, you establish the pecking order of your life, by classifying who is above you and who is below you based on what you see that they project. Hence, you will need to get rid of your initial knowledge on what it is to be an Alpha. If you do this, and reinvent the way you see other people, then we can release The Alpha in You.

According to Dr. Kate Ludeman and Dr. Eddie Erlandson, there are four types of Alpha Males. They are:

- The **COMMANDERS**: The great leaders, trendsetters, intense characters, and source of inspiration.

- The **VISIONARIES**: The curious, imaginative, intuitive, expansive, future-oriented.

- The **STRATEGISTS**: The calculative, methodical, brilliant, fact-oriented, data dependent, analytic, sharp, and systematic thinkers.

- The **EXECUTORS**: The hardworking, tireless, disciplined, strong, persevering, goal-oriented, with a sharp eye for details.

A true Alpha Male have all these 4 characteristics whether learned or by nature.

11 Traits of an Alpha Male

Let's start now! I am going to be giving you a series of traits, behaviors, and attitudes an evolved man adapts in order to become the Alpha. Stop wasting away your energy in petty envy. Start focusing on yourself! Are you ready?

1 - HELPFUL — but NOT Condescending

An Alpha aims for success, but it does not mean he acquires tunnel vision and forgets he now has influence over other people surrounding him. Helping others should also become an Alpha's core value.

Remember, people become successful when they surround themselves with other successful people. To do this, the Alpha must also play his part to contribute to others' success. However, responsibility lies on the Alpha to not overextend his bounds and make helping counterproductive. An Alpha aims to help others grow, not make them dependent.

2 - CONFIDENT — But Not Cocky

The old model of an Alpha is known to be cocky and rises through ranks by stepping on other people. By lowering the value of other people, he raises his own through exaggeration of talents he does not have or undermining the contribution of others. Thus, this Alpha is only strong by maintaining others' delusion of his capacities.

A true Alpha is confident because he knows his skills and his limits. He is confident because he can rely on others for skills he does not have. He is confident that these people will remain loyal to him because he appreciates their value and acknowledges their strengths.

3 - VAIN — But Not Conceited

Research has found that attractive men make more money in their work and earn higher positions. An Alpha should maintain a good sense of self-image but not to the point of conceit. By looking good, the Alpha feels good. By feeling good, the Alpha radiates this positive energy to others around him, improving his interaction with other people.

4 - PRIDEFUL — But Not Arrogant

A best-selling author once quoted that arrogance is the combination of pride and ignorance. An Alpha always aspires to know all, and never act when in the lack of knowledge. However, in the event of success, the Alpha shares this with other people through his pride, in the hopes that such an act will inspire success for others as well.

5 - HUMBLE — But Not Self-Loathing

An Alpha should learn humility. This humility will fuel the Alpha's hunger to strive for more. However, the Alpha understands the bounds of humility and should learn to appreciate successes. Too much humility will lead to self-loathing, which is against the principles an Alpha strives for.

6 - TOLERANT — But Not Weak

Life is hard and being an Alpha doesn't exempt you. Life will push people around.

When this happens, some give up and others try to fight back hard only to get tired and give up as well. An Alpha should be tolerant to the hardships of life, but that does not give him an excuse to be weak. The Alpha accepts how life will push him around. He will try to ride that wave and manipulate it to his advantage.

7 - DEDICATED — But Not Obsessed

An Alpha is dedicated to his work, but he is also dedicated to his family, friends, and his health. The perfect balance must be maintained. Should the Alpha sway slightly between these facets in his life, he becomes obsessed. By maintaining proper balance, the Alpha grows holistically and becomes a role model to the workaholic, the family man, the happy-go-lucky friends, and to the overly cautious.

8 - HE SPEAKS — But Also Listens

The Alpha male is never shy to speak out. He should have the necessary confidence it takes to speak to a group of people.

Research shows that 1 out of 5 people find death a better alternative rather than having to speak in front of a crowd. The Alpha male does not shy away from attention and projects his voice in such a manner that a crowd becomes moved by what he is saying. Such a power should only belong to a responsible individual -- a trait an Alpha male already possesses.

An Alpha male is not only the man giving orders, but he is also the man who listens to the concerns of the crowd. He collates all that he knows from those who surround him and speaks for the whole of the group when the time comes. In short, the Alpha male is what binds a group's communication together.

9 - COURAGEOUS — But not reckless

To be an Alpha Male, one has to be courageous so he can do things lesser men would shy away from. An Alpha Male leads a pack. In such sense, he has to make decisions for a group, and not all decisions are easy.

Lesser men would shirk off responsibility in fear of having to make choices, which would affect the group. As such, lesser men are susceptible to suboptimal performance and lack of achievement.

An Alpha Male is not afraid of responsibility, and therefore is not afraid to make big decisions that affect other people's lives. As such, he is courageous. An Alpha Male can make correct choices under pressure and stress, but never do so when he knows he lacks the proper information or time. As such, he is not reckless.

10 - OMNISCIENT — But not a deity

To be omniscient means to be able to see everything, but this is not meant in the level of a deity. An Alpha Male needs to be all seeing in the sense that he has to look at all factors, ins and outs, alternatives, and variables to a problem or situation. He must be willing to look at something others turn a blind eye on. He must be willing to not only think outside the box but also consider the box and how it was made. If you decide to see everything, then you will know more than the average man and you will make better decisions. Judging from the fact the Alpha decides to see and know all he can, his courage and confidence are better fueled.

When an Alpha Male decides to be all seeing, he never presumes he is at level with a higher being. He must always keep in mind that he is a man, and is always prone to mistakes.

Such knowledge will keep him careful and to always double check his steps. If he decides to think he is at level with a deity, then he will have already lost his Alpha Male status to cockiness.

11- TEACHER — But also a learner

Once someone has become an Alpha Male in the minds of other people, these people will subconsciously look up to the Alpha for guidance. People will slowly come to the Alpha for questions and concerns. When this happens, the Alpha has a great responsibility to teach the proper methods and techniques to handle a problem, or whatever the situation calls for.

Since it has fallen to the Alpha to become a teacher, he has to be responsible for what he has to say. And to do this, the Alpha needs to be a learner as well. The Alpha absorbs all he can from the world surrounding him and relays all this knowledge at the right place and the right time. When he finds something difficult, he goes out of his way to find opportunities to deal with that problem again until he has mastered the solution. Lesser men would run the opposite direction of something they don't know how to do. Alpha Males charge on and face these problems with a smile and a ready heart. In that, he is a learner.

In other words, to be an Alpha male, a man must develop his character holistically. He cannot sway or linger with one trait, but must make sure that all are developed together. Otherwise, he will become lopsided like a mutated animal. In a pack of wolves, not one of them will look up to a leader who is anything but perfect. An Alpha male cannot be too kind, but must make sure to be a balance of kindness and firmness. An Alpha male cannot be too iron-fisted, but must be a balance between hardness and gentleness.

Lastly, an Alpha male is not one who cares about what others think of him, but what he can do for others. The old model of an Alpha male focuses on trying to fabricate an image into people's minds and depend on that image for power. The real Alpha male is someone who leads by example and generates a genuine image of power in other people's minds through no effort other than by authentic leadership. He knows that what others think of him is none of his business. Because of this, he minds his own business and enriches other people as he does so. In other words, an Alpha male is someone who does not work hard to become Alpha to other people's eyes, but one who works hard to develop himself as an Alpha in his own eyes.

Are you ready to do what it takes to become an Alpha Male?

CHAPTER 2: HOW TO BE AN ALPHA MALE?

In order to reach an answer, we must first go through a solution. Just like everything else in life, all things are done through a proper formula. Hence, there are steps one simply needs to make in order to develop his being and become an Alpha Male.

7 Steps How to be an Alpha Male

If you are ready, take the next steps one by one. Becoming an Alpha Male does not happen overnight. It needs focus, constant practice, and repetition.

Here are the steps:

STEP 1: Visualization

In your mind's eye, imagine looking at yourself as an Alpha Male.

Having a hard time?

This is normal, especially when you haven't started shaping your character. One good exercise I can recommend is to take out a pen and paper. Now, take a look at yourself and list down all the things you have that an Alpha Male shouldn't have. Fold that paper and keep it somewhere you'll never lose like a jewelry box, your piggy bank, or in the drawer where you keep all your important documents and never look at it again. This will be your "before" mental image, which is like the same thing when someone snaps a picture of themselves before they start a weight loss program.

On the other hand, if you had an easy time imagining yourself to be an Alpha Male, this means you've already started your journey to becoming one subconsciously and will just need proper refinement.

STEP 2: Be confident

Are you aware that in order for you to go to sleep, you actually have to pretend to be asleep until you actually do? This is the same advice to people who lack confidence. If you are not confident, pretend that you are and the rest will follow.

Men and women respond to someone who is confident and questions those they can see who are not. If you talk to a group with a slouched posture, stumble on your words, and with a blank face, nobody will believe you. You can't blame people for judging you this way because everybody else can see that you don't even believe in yourself.

Confidence arises from loving yourself and being sure of what you can do. If you appreciate what you can offer and you are sure you have a wide base of what you know, it will show with your body language, and it, in turn, will signal your audience that this man is confident. So, how do you become confident? Study your craft and refine your techniques. Never go into something unprepared, no matter how good you are. If you still doubt yourself and can't find confidence even when you are well prepared, then do what a person who wants to sleep does. Pretend. Everything else will follow.

STEP 3: Improve your Posture

"Back straight! Chin up!" This is what you usually hear when a staff sergeant is drilling his new recruits. Even as a kid, your mother would continually fuss over your posture. But what's so good about good posture and how does it make you an Alpha Male?

According to a study done back in January 2011, good body posture activates the sense of power within the mind, allowing people to feel and behave like they are in charge. Psychologically, it also makes the person more trustworthy than talking to a man slouching and stumbling on his words.

There are many different kinds of posture. An Alpha Male should present an "open posture", which is represented by separated feet, head straight, palms up, and fingers slightly spread apart. Literally, the Alpha Male is exposing all of his vulnerable body parts as a sign that he is peaceful, friendly, and does not consider anything a threat. Psychologically, people will view this as a great sign of confidence and power.

On the other hand, if you present a "closed posture", such as arms across the chest, hands clasped in front of the genitals, or crossing of legs denotes a man who is defensive, fearful, hostile, or disinterested and should not be what an Alpha Male presents.

STEP 4: Listen more than you talk

An Alpha Male is someone who absorbs all he can possibly know so he can apply everything he has learned at the right place and time. When an Alpha Male opens his mouth to speak, it must always be because he has substance to share. As such, the Alpha Male is not someone anybody can call shallow, narrow-minded, or misinformed. Due to the fact that the Alpha male always says something of substance, people will start to listen to him with a ready ear because they are used to always find something useful as to what he has to say.

In order to gain information, an Alpha Male needs to be a good listener. To become a good listener means he is not there to listen for the sake of creating the image of a listener, but because he is there to acquire information, digest it, and store it for future use. One technique of good listening, a manager once taught me was, "If your employees come to tell you something, listen with a passive face and no reaction whatsoever. This will make them uncomfortable and decide to tell you more than they initially intended." This is a powerful tool that managers use to get the most information from reluctant subordinates. Do not feel bad if you think this is a psychological manipulation, since you are not doing anything but listening. However, appreciate the fact that it is proven to be effective.

STEP 5: Seek to Do That Which You Fear

An Alpha Male should not shy away from responsibility, even it that responsibility means doing something you dread or hate. Psychologically, people fear things that they do not know (or know how to do). It is like a particularly difficult job at work that everybody tries to pass around until it's dropped off at the weakest person's desk. Things are only difficult if you do not wish to learn the proper way of doing it. Once a person knows the proper way of doing it, the human ingenuity takes over and will find a way of doing it in an easier and timely manner. Some business owners I know jokingly say that they like hiring lazy people because if you give a lazy person a job to do, they'll always find the easiest way of doing it.

An Alpha Male should get out of their way to face things they do not desire and keep doing it until they find it as a really easy job to do. If there's a task at work that everybody avoids like the plague, the Alpha Male should be the first one to volunteer to do that project and lead by example, showing everyone that it's not that difficult.

STEP 6: Get In Shape

Believe me, this is a bit hard. Unlike other steps where you try to develop a character, this is developing a whole new lifestyle. For some people, it may take close to a year (or even more), for others, it may be as easy as changing clothes. And, no, getting in shape does not mean getting six-pack abs, toned biceps, and muscular legs. It's about gaining the proper body mass index or attaining the proper weight for your height and body frame.

Getting in shape starts with discipline. If there's one thing I earned from joining the varsity swimming team in my college years, it wasn't only the medals, but also the discipline. It takes discipline to say no to overindulgence of food and discipline to get up off the couch and exercise. Without discipline, any exercise and diet regimen you start now is doomed to fail the moment you lose your sudden inspiration to start.

So, start slowly. If your regular meal is two servings of carbs (rice, mashed potatoes, or what have you), then maybe you can slowly cut it down to one and a half this week then down to one a week after. Just like how a smoker quits smoking. They don't quit overnight, but gradually do it in a span of months.

What does getting in shape have anything to do with being an Alpha Male? Studies have shown that attractive men make more money and earn higher positions. At the same time, they are a pleasure to deal with and interactions with such men are always a pleasure. Also, it's a bit hard trying to inspire discipline into the people who look up to you when they see you don't have the discipline to keep your body in shape.

STEP 7: Have a Thirst for Reading

If you're reading this book, then I'll know you've already accomplished this step. Reading is fundamental to everything in this day and age. Vast amounts of information can be read almost anywhere - from newspapers, books, web pages, or even in social media. An Alpha Male requires you to know a little about a lot. Reading books will help you to achieve this.

At one point in my life, I felt I was not managing my funds very well. What I did was I picked up a book focused on financial education and it opened my eyes to whole new concepts and ideas that would greatly help the way I managed my savings. I never looked back and I applied everything I learned from a single book.

Now, I can proudly say my investment portfolio is not empty and if anyone were to ask me concepts about financial planning, I'd answer them in a heartbeat.

There are a lot of brilliant people out there, and we're very lucky if we can meet them and have them teach us all they know. But why would you need to do that when you can always grab a copy of their book and read.

CHAPTER 3: BETA MALE TRAITS YOU MUST AVOID

It's so easy to spot Beta Males all around us. Sometimes, they could even be us! Believe me, you DO NOT want to be caught with the following traits. In the following chapter, if you feel you exhibit one or more of the following traits, you'd better get them out of your system. You DO NOT want to be a Beta Male.

5 Traits of a Beta Male

1 - Bad Posture

People tend to know who's dominant in a crowd just by looking at a person's posture. As discussed earlier, an Alpha Male knows how to stand and sit, with an open posture exuding friendliness, calm, and peace. He knows he is under no threat to life or ego, and thus his body shows the openness to the world and people around him.

A Beta Male, on the other hand, is guarded, defensive, and fearful. He is afraid of how others will judge him when they see him enter the room, or the impending ridicule when they have to address a crowd. Thus, his body posture shows such manifestations of his insecurities.

The following are bad posture practices that you should ALWAYS avoid as an Alpha Male:

• Avoiding Eye Contact

People who avoid eye contact cannot be trusted. They say that the eyes are the windows to the soul. Thus, when a man avoids eye contact, people tend to feel that he is hiding something and fear that others will find out when they "look through the windows" and lay bare his lie.

- ## Hands Covering Genital Area / Crossing your Knees

As part of the animal kingdom, one of our primal instincts is to protect the part of our body that allows us to procreate and spread our progeny. Thus, when Beta Males subconsciously shift their posture to have their hands cover their genital areas, this is a telltale sign that he is guarding himself against something he deems as a threat (an intimidating boss or an overly attractive woman), which is what a weak person would do. An Alpha Male cannot be intimidated by such people, and thus, always exudes an open posture.

- ## Crossed Arms

Similar to protecting the genital areas from a threat, a man who crosses his arms across his chest is defensive and a subconscious way of the body trying to protect its vital organs from harm. Only a weak Beta Male finds threats where there is none through his weakness and paranoia.

• Sitting on the Edge of a Chair

A Beta Male who sits on the edge of a chair shows he is apprehensive and might as well tell the whole room that he would rather get up and leave. This is usually because of anxiety the room or meeting is causing him making his mind scream, "Fly, you fool!"

2 - Submissive Attitude

A man who always bows to other men will never be an Alpha Male. The whole life of a submissive Beta Male is revolved into kissing asses in the attempt of getting to the top. Both you and I know that no amount of courting your boss will ever get you his job. "Promotion" is a lie that employers dangle at our faces so we act like good little puppets and dance to their tune, making us work hard for a sliver of a chance at that promotion. It's exactly like those cartoon shows we used to watch when we were kids where a stubborn and lazy donkey would walk by dangling a piece of carrot in front of him from a stick.

Another great example nature shows us about being a submissive Beta Male can be found in a team of sled dogs in the frozen reaches of the Earth. While doing a sled run, the second dog (the beta) will always stare at the first dog's (the alpha) asshole.

This is how it's going to be for the rest of that dog's life until he shows his master that he is the real alpha. Only then will he be allowed to lead the team. This is exactly the same for men all over the world. There is a pecking order to things, and it's up to you how high you want to perch.

Being submissive is a great manifestation of a Beta Male's lack of confidence, low self-esteem, and inferiority complex. These three are the exact opposite of what an Alpha Male's traits should be. Nature did not intend man to be submissive. When we were living like animals before civilization, man had to hunt for food or die. Nature culled the human race through natural selection by eliminating the weak and retaining the strong. Those who cannot hunt (Beta Males) would die, taking their Beta Male genes with them to the grave. While those who were fearless and conquered the challenge of life survived long enough to reproduce and spread their Alpha Male genes for the future of mankind. If Mother Nature was a person, she'd be shaking her head and wondering how this new breed of weak and submissive Beta Males came to be.

3 - Poor Communicator

One does not have to be a genius in order to communicate, but only Alpha Males communicate well. People who stutter and stumble on their words show a severe lack of self-confidence, the main trait of a Beta Male.

Stuttering may be a medical condition to some people (they say people who stutter have minds that think so fast that their tongues are unable to catch up), but to those who stutter AND have slow wit at the same time will always be a Beta Male.

Good communication comes from a good confidence level. Like we mentioned from the previous chapters, confidence comes from proper preparation (no matter how good you are), proper knowledge, and self-acceptance. If you lack any one of the three, you will never be truly confident, and thus, stumble or mumble when asked to talk to a crowd.

There was this one point in my life where I realized my communication skills were going down the drain. It was when I was depressed that my self-confidence slowly ebbed away. Until one day, I was waiting in line at the local Starbucks and I noticed the staff taking the orders always greeted the customer with a smile and a loud, clear voice. Some people mumbled back their orders and I realized the Alpha in the situation was the Starbucks staff. It became really funny to look at after that, when I noticed the next customer, a businessman in a suit, mumbled his order at the spritely staff and was slouching with head bowed as he was handing the cashier his payment. Then it dawned on me: people who openly display their Alpha Male traits (the Starbucks staff in this situation) sends subliminal messages to everyone else in the room that he is the Alpha.

In response to this subliminal insinuation, people with a dominant Beta Male character dances to the Alpha's tune and shows him the respect his status is due. And all of this is happening without anyone noticing but me! So, when it was my turn to make my order, I stood up straight, head held high, smiled and greeted the staff with a loud, clear voice and made my order. The staff started to show signs of reverence when he handed me my change with two hands, offered that I take a seat, and wait at my table where a barista will deliver my drink. In my mind, I was just getting my Alpha back. In the cashier's mind, he was dealing with a very important person, for what kind of person could make an established Alpha bow. In his mind, I was a lead dog.

4 - Panicky

A Beta Male is a person who easily gets stressed and panics. This is because of an attitude rooted in pessimism and automatically viewing sudden changes negatively. An Alpha Male always stays optimistic and rides the waves. An Alpha Male tolerates being pushed around by life, but he contorts his body so that he is pushed to the desired place. A Beta Male is someone who curls up into a ball and lets life push him around. A Beta Male is someone who swims against the waves, gets tired, and drowns. So, when there is a problem, a Beta Male becomes stressed, panics, and fails.

However, an Alpha Male tries to understand why it is a problem, looks for all solutions and possible outcomes, and makes the choice that will benefit him the most.

Beta Males guiding principle in life is "everything is going to work out", while an Alpha Male's guiding principle when it comes to problems is "problems are a part of life as the air we breathe". So when a Beta Male encounters a problem, he gets angry, refuses to solve the problem, and runs away because he keeps thinking that everything is supposed to work out. Hence, they will always be in denial of a presented problem. However, when an Alpha Male finds a problem, he remains calm and he sits down, analyzes it, gets help, and finds the solution. He expects problems and knows they are a part of life, so problems never come to him in a surprise. Thus, he never panics.

5 - Lacks Responsibility

Beta Males do not want to take any responsibility more than they have to. They are the type of people who have a copy of their Job Description in their desk and take it out every time their boss asks them to do something just to make sure the chore is part of their job responsibility.

Beta Males also do not want to assume the responsibility of anything. So when something goes wrong and company demands someone to pin it on, the Beta Male is the first one to point a finger. Seriously, if you and a Beta Male was running from a bear and he was holding a gun with only 1 bullet, he'd shoot you in the leg and leave you to distract the bear in fear that his one bullet may not be enough to stop a rampaging animal.

A Beta Male always lives in fear of things that get in the way of their comfort cocoon, and responsibilities are one of them. They do not realize that responsibilities will always be their burden either from a conscious choice of deciding to pick it up, or when they are pushed to a corner and forced to carry a responsibility (i.e. finding out you're a dad when the kid's 5 years old only because the mother died and there's nobody else to take care of the child. Sounds like an Adam Sandler movie script). An Alpha Male accepts responsibilities as a part of life and is always ready to jump in and manage an obligation because he knows it is what makes him a better man.

If you keep doing the same thing over and over, and never take chances to carry new obligations, then you will get stuck in a boring routine and live a very boring life. What's more is you will never grow as a person and get stuck in that cocoon you love so much now, but will despise in the future.

It's not a surprise why Beta Males who grow too old always regret their choices and wished they lived a different life, but only when it's already too late.

Responsibility molds character and makes boys into men.

CHAPTER 4: HOW TO ATTRACT WOMEN

When you get employed, your boss will not ask you to go deal with their biggest VIP client on your first day. On your first game after joining the basketball team, your coach won't trust you to make the final game-winning play. On your first day in professional boxing, you don't go knock on Manny Pacquiao's door and challenge him to a fight.

The point we're trying to get here is that you never do something big without the proper instruction, training, and exposure. In short, you need solid fundamentals. The same concept applies when you want to attract women. If people didn't need good fundamentals to attract women, then I would make this the first chapter, instead of the fourth, and save everybody else's time.

Attracting women require you to develop and establish all the skills and attitudes explained in chapter 1 and 2, and get rid of all the bad traits discussed in chapter 3. Once you've done this, or at least started to, then proceed to follow these golden and timely tips on how to attract women.

a. DO: Things You Should Practice Regularly

Become an Alpha Male
All traits embodied by an Alpha Male can attract women. Sometimes, you don't even have to talk or look your best. Your reputation will be enough to win her interest in a heartbeat. Confidence, responsibility, great posture, and being superb at talking are all traits that make women's heads turn.

1 - Look Good

Let's face it: not all men are born equal. Some of us are tall, but others lack the height. Others have skin so smooth, while the rest of us have it dull. However, being born with an aesthetic disadvantage does not mean you are automatically a loser. There are other parts of the human body that can attract women other than a pretty face, and believe me when I say not all women base their attraction on a man's face alone.

Get in shape! You don't need expensive equipment or a gym membership to start exercising. Pretend you're in a prison and use your body's weight + gravity as your exercising tool. Do push-ups, crunches, pull-ups, jog, or jump. Lastly, stick to a diet.

Wear great clothes! Have you ever seen an ugly man wear an awesome suit? I've seen a lot and I've seen women stare. Wearing great fashion or clothes is one way to attract the ladies. You don't need a pretty face when you've got a great fashion sense!

2 - Get Financial Education & Become Financially Stable

I am not saying women are gold-diggers. However, women will look at your investment portfolio if given the chance, and take this is a positive sign! Allow me to explain.

Women would never attach themselves to a man who is financially unstable. Financial instability shows women that a man is not financially educated, does not know how to manage his cash flow, and does not know how to make investments. When you lack these important skills, a woman knows you are not capable providing for a family and children. You can't even provide for yourself! And that's why I mentioned it's a positive sign when women take an interest in your stability since it's a sign that they want a good future for your future family (if you get married).

However, not all women are angels. You should still be vigilant against gold-digging, soul-sucking, life-draining people out there. But then again, an Alpha Male would never fall to the wiles of a manipulative partner.

3 - Branding

I am not saying you'll need to get the latest Louis Vuitton wallet or wear an Armani suit every day. What we mean here is to create YOUR brand. The BRAND of YOU. When we say "brand", it often comes hand in hand with a general object. For example, think of a brand of a car? A cologne brand? A dishwasher brand?

How about a brand of you? How do you make yourself a brand so that when women think "responsible", they think of you? When women think "successful", your smiling face comes in mind?

In order to make yourself a brand, you will need to become an Alpha Male. Once you have established that, you have to excel in whatever job you have. Each achievement, each congratulatory comment on your social networking page, and each certificate you receive add points to your brand. So, the moment women mention your name, only positive attributes come with it. That is how you should be branded.

4 - Be Funny or Be Interesting

You don't have to be the best stand-up comedian to woo a woman. Too much humor makes you a clown. Nobody wants to date a clown (sorry, clowns). So, administer humor in proper dosages.

If you really can't crack a joke, then be interesting. You don't have to be mysterious or be shady just to pique a girl's interest. You also don't need to make up stories, or else you'll come out as a bragging little brat. BE HONEST. There was this one time I was really down in my life (about to get laid off, lots of bills to pay, no backup plan), and I poured my heart out to this girl I was dating.

The topics were interesting and the emotions were real. Women love that. We've been together for five years now. Oh, and I found a new job after that, so she still took me in.

b. DON'T: Things You Should <u>NOT</u> Do

1 - Don't Look Like You Just Got Up from Bed

Women do not like haggard-looking men. Yes, a stubble looks sexy and adds to that "dirty-look" charm, but only when paired with a sleek suit, not a graying white shirt and boxers!

If you just got off from work and want to go to a bar to pick up girls, don't loosen your shirt or take off your tie to "relax". Keep them on. If you dress to impress your boss, you should do the same to attract women.

Lastly, if you're going out on a date, always follow this checklist:

1. Take a bath
Even if you already took one this morning! If you can smell your armpits, then so can everybody else these past four hours!

2. Trim your beard.
If you don't have one, shave off the stubble.

3. Shave your balls.
You never know what the night brings.

4. Wear your best clothes.
Assume you're going out to die and you don't want to be caught dead wearing last month's fashion.

5. Comb your hair.
Don't go for that "wacky" hairdo. Make it clean and formal. You don't want your nickname to be "that-guy-with-the-weird-hairstyle". And for God's sakes, don't apply too much product!

6. Wear your best scent.
Spray in designated areas: neck, left chest, right chest, on the wrists, rub together, and wipe behind the ears.

7. DO NOT wear sunglasses if your date is indoors.

You won't look cool. You'll look like an asshole.

2 - Don't Ask if She Has a Boyfriend

Seriously, DO NOT do this. It's like finding a gun and using it on yourself. There are better ways to kill a future relationship with a woman. The only acceptable time to ask a woman this is if it's clear that she's very interested in you and you guys are going to the next level, but NOT when you've just met her or when you're still having your first drink.

3 - Don't Be Boring

Dead air is bad on TV, and it's certainly bad in a conversation with a woman. When you're running out of things to say, turn the conversation over to her. Women like to talk, especially about themselves. So, ask them about her family, work, interests, and whatever comes to mind. Make sure when she's talking that you are listening because women have a knack of remembering things they told you and getting upset when you can't remember.

CHAPTER 5: COMMUNICATE LIKE AN ALPHA MALE

Too many men are focused on the small details such as hairstyles or what colors to wear. While in this case, when it comes to communicating, men are too enthralled about the best line to say or dropping a clever line at the perfect moment. My friend, if this is you, then you are you not going to go anywhere with women. It's your voice what people hear and not so much what are the exact words you use. Simple concept: No matter what you say, if you say it softly you will be ignored (unless you are an influential person), while if you say it in a high-quality tone of voice you will be listened to.

a. The Tone of Your Voice

This is mainly about how you say things. This includes the volume of your voice, the speed of how fast you speak and the **tone** you use. Your voice tone will be our mood setter, giving you the ability to come off as an Alpha Male or nervous and weak like most men out there. Through your voice you will be able to:

- Display how you feel about yourself. Either you feel confident, nervous, shy, sexual, funny, etc...

- Give people who hear you the chance to judge you as an Alpha or not (although it doesn't matter.)

- Gain respect from your peers around, or even strangers depending on where you are.

- Woo a woman and influence her mental image of you to be an Alpha Male, even before she sees you physically.

b. How People Communicate

Communication among people is all around us and communication around the world is all the same. Try this, go in the middle of a somewhat populated area (the lobby of your University or office building) and just look around. How do they communicate?

You will observe:

- Smiles left and right or a simple nod of the head.

- A quick hello or deep and long conversations.

- Laughter! There's a saying "You can make a woman laugh all the way to bed."

- Storytelling or asking questions.

You will see these behaviors in all people all around the world. People are communicating at all times everywhere. The only differences are the languages, but a loud voice in French is also a loud voice in Japanese. If both are loud then both are Alpha. Through this concept, it may be easy to see that you will be able to attract women from almost every corners of the world solely using your voice.

Humans speak in different tones. Using body language (hands, face or even their actual whole body) to express themselves as they speak. Some use more hands and less voice, others solely their voice and few are simply silently loud through how expressive they are using movement. This is the point of communication, to express yourself. If you are pissed then express it, if you are happy then show it and if you are in love or any other emotion you feel then you NEED to express it without hesitation. This is how an Alpha Male communicates and this is what attracts women and makes men respect you. Now that I have explained tonality and why it is so important, let's show you how to obtain it.

c. What Makes the Tone of the Alpha Male

- Deep and smooth voice

- Speak slowly

- Be direct

Most men will have at least a small problem with all three. Some will have more problems than others, so let's begin. Everyone has two voices, our high sounds will come from our "head voice" while our lower ones come from your "chest voice."

We want to always speak with our chest voice. A quick tip is to say "Do you want to the party with me?" then say it again while closing your nose with your fingers, if there's no difference in the sound then you are already speaking with your chest voice and no need to be paranoid about if you are speaking like an Alpha or not. If you voice becomes nasally then you are speaking with your voice and you need to practice.

Probably one of the biggest problems men have is that they speak too fast. This is because we are brought up learning to say what we have to say as soon as possible or else people will get bored and stop paying attention to us when it is the exact opposite that is true. If your body language is right and your tonality is as well, then you'll be an interesting Alpha Male that women would love to listen to. So say it slowly to avoid a "What?!" or a more polite "Can you say that again please?"

Now being direct is something many young men do not do. We are always trying to make what we say creative and interesting when in reality going straight to the point is the best way, let me give you an example.

"I used to like live in Cali and I just didn't really uh like it there. The people there weren't nice and they hard to like talk to. I would go to like the plazas and stuff to talk to people. It's wasn't like my hometown where people were always like nice."

"I used to live in California and I didn't enjoy living there. I found the people shallow and hard to communicate with, unlike my hometown."

The first statement seems drawn out, boring and overall uninteresting while our second statement it direct and straight to the point where nothing is missing nor nothing is unnecessarily added on. Avoid word fillers such as "uh" or "like." You always want to get your point across as direct and clear as possible. Not as *fast* as possible but as **direct** as possible.

d. How to Behave like an Alpha Male

Alphas will show certain characteristics in the way behave and how they communicate. I'll give you guys some examples of these characteristics which are pretty obvious to interpret. That's the one thing I want you to have in your head, which these characteristics aren't rocket science but just normal behaviors any nice person would have.

1 - Speak Loudly:

If you are having a conversation with someone and you are not speaking loudly then the person who you are speaking to will lose interest, obvious. Unless they are extremely interested what you have to say then you will be fine but you will have just normal conversations with. To be on the safe side, speak loudly.

2 - Be Entertaining:

This is one is pretty obvious too. Who wants to watch a boring documentary compared to a great action movie? The Same concept applies here, do not be that the boring documentary but be the entertaining movie that everyone loves. This can be done by talking about thought-provoking controversial topics, do not be afraid to step on anyone's shoes because that will be entertaining. Not our normal every day "What did you do today?" conversation.

3 - Tell Stories:

Use stories to get people interested, especially funny or awkward moments in your life, dramatic stories do well also. As long as the stories will manipulate emotion. If you are trying to get a point across then using metaphors will make your point easier to understand as well entertaining.

4 - Has a good range of vocabulary:

Using a good vocabulary will have a great psychological effect on people. You will seem like an educated person who respects and well cultured. This language can tell a lot about a person, you can tell if a man is an Alpha Male or not.

e. Body Language Tips

1- Take Up Space:

An Alpha male will not be hesitant to take up space due to their nature to dominate the area they are in. An example of this is when standing, you should keep your feet about shoulder width apart. While in presentation, walk around the room to show you own it.

2 - Move at a Slow Pace:

If you turn your head quickly, dash wherever you go or are all jittery with your hands then the message you will send to those around you will be "I am a nervous man who needs to get out of where I am ASAP." We want to be relaxed and in control of our movements. An Alpha Male is never in a hurry because they are always in control of their time and environment. Chill out and stay relaxed. It will then be shown in your body movement.

3 - Always Keep your Hands Visible:

If others can see your hands then you will come off as a non-threatening Alpha (We don't want to scare anyone.) Why do you think the open hand "hello" is so popular and welcoming? Hands within the pockets will give the vibe of a nervous or disinterested man.

As an alternative, use your hands while speaking to others. This will make whatever you say look more important.

4 - Touch:

Touching someone in a non-sexual way (or sexual way too!) is a great way to make someone feel comfortable around you. Now no need to go overboard and touch the person everywhere or constantly, a simple rub on the arm or a two handed (refer to how many politicians shake hands) will do wonders to how a person will feel around you. Hugs, high fives, and slight taps on the shoulders are enough to get your message across, that you are a strong Alpha Male who isn't fazed by anyone.

5 - Eye Contact:

Let's set up a bar scenario with two men, Guy #1 and Guy #2. Guy #1 is sitting with his drink hunched backed, is making no eye contact with people, is not being social at all and when he is, he does not speak up. Right from my description anyone will be able to tell that this man is not an Alpha at all. In a real life situation, these signs may not be as obvious but everyone will always sense a somewhat of a bad vibe from him.

Let's set up a bar scenario with two men, Guy #1 and Guy #2. Guy #1 is sitting with his drink hunched backed, is making no eye contact with people, is not being social at all and when he is, he does not speak up. Right from my description anyone will be able to tell that this is man is not an Alpha at all.

In a real life situation these signs may not be as obvious but everyone will always sense a somewhat of a bad vibe from him.

Now Guy #2 is sitting at the bar with good posture, strong eye contact with everyone, talks a whole lot, speaks up when he has to say something and in general is taking up space. Our Guy #2 is our Alpha Male. He is a man of high value and interest where for all we know he could be a garbage man but will not change his Alpha Male attitude. Using the same concept, Guy #1 could be a millionaire with an amazing car and beautiful bedroom but with his Beta-like characteristics, he won't be bringing any ladies into his car and certainly into his bedroom.

I hope after reading you have now a better idea how an Alpha Male communicates. He will use pauses and speak slowly in his speech and body language that will be shown through his posture, eye contact and overall relaxed nature to let everyone else in his vicinity know who the Alpha Male is.

CHAPTER 6: ACT LIKE AN ALPHA MALE

Being an Alpha Male is actually a very simple concept. Many men in modern times are too preoccupied with their hairstyles, whether or not to keep clean nails or the most Adonis-like body obtainable. Now I'm not saying these aren't all attractive traits in a man, they just aren't what make YOU attractive. They simply carry themselves however they want, without second-guessing. This is what makes you attractive. Now you have to DECIDE to become an Alpha Male or not, it's a choice and everyone can become one. At first, it will be difficult and at times awkward but it's a habit that has to be learned.

Now let's get into the specifics. It's the small differences that will separate an Alpha Male from the normal men. Many times we will not be able to pinpoint what exactly makes a man so damn attractive (neither can women) they just have "it", all we end up saying is "Wow! He looks great!" It is all about their body language and behavior. Some are born this way and others learn to find it within themselves. Every man can become successful with women and garner more respect from their peers by making simple adjustments to their body language and behavior.

Let's now describe what an Alpha Male is. Some answers thrown around will be the most seductive, others will say the most confident, a leader who will loudly display his dominance or a very popular answer, the best looking one. Now this all true, but not the whole big picture. You do NOT need to handsome or extremely good looking to be an Alpha Male. Many good-looking guys just don't have "it." Constantly falling into the friendzone or other males does not take them seriously. On the other side of the spectrum, you will find men who are not good looking at all yet much more successful than their handsome counterparts. Why is this? Because being an Alpha Male is a mindset.

Females find Alpha Males attractive and why is this? Women have a special sixth sense that they have developed over millions of years of evolution. It gives them the ability to understand body language and find a valuable partner. It's all in the way you carry yourself, this will send signals to everyone around him that he is the leader, the strongest man and importantly the most valuable in the group.

Luckily enough, an Alpha Male lives inside us all, and the ladies will melt when you bring out to the open. Remember, everything is sub communicated through body language. Many studies, most popular one being from American psychologist Ray Birdwhistell, state that in conversation only 1/3 of all information comes from words while 2/3 come from subtle body language. Your mannerisms speak very loudly friend, and we can all hear them loud and clear.

a. How to Stand like an Alpha Male

Stand in front of a mirror large enough to see your entire body and ask yourself "Do I look like an Alpha Male?" Try and see if just by you simply standing you are expressing you masculinity or if you are displaying confidence. If it's a no, then here are few tips to help you out.

1 - Stand up Straight and Bring your Chest Out:

This is giving off the message that you are not afraid to attack or to be attacked.

2 - Display your Sexuality:

Done by having your legs a little wider than shoulder width. It will help give you a solid and masculine look.

3 - Straighten your Neck:

Keeping your head up and looking straight will give you a little more height and show others you are not afraid of confrontation. NEVER look away from people, at your feet or theirs.

4 - Exercise:

Is will give you a better posture as well as a wider figure. You will also feel great and full of energy that will aid your overall Alpha Male aura.

b. How to Walk like an Alpha Male

Whether in the office, on the streets or in your favorite bar, your walk will say a lot about yourself and be considered as a first impression to many. Here's some advice to help make your walk as Alpha Male as possible.

1 - Walk slowly:

This is will show that you are not afraid when you enter a room. Simply relax and take time with every step you take.

2 - Shoulder length Steps:

Steps that are too short will make you look feminine or like a follower.

On the hand, steps that are too wide will make you look clumsy and not in control. Shoulder length steps are the ideal distance your feet should be traveling.

3 - Smile:

Smiles are contagious. Seeing a happy man walking down the street smiling will spread this feeling everywhere he goes.

c. How to Sit like an Alpha Male

Men will spend a decent amount of time sitting down (I am currently seated while writing this) and you can bet that even seated an Alpha Male can be seen from a mile away. Here's how they do it.

1 - Sit Straight and Comfortably:

Take up as much space as you think you will need. Look relaxed and remember that one reason why we sit is because we're tired of standing.

2 - Show your Torso:

Lean back and show off your chest. Make sure you feel comfortable and it will show that you are not afraid of confrontation.

3 - Do Not Close Yourself Off:

This includes crossing your arms across your chest or bringing out knees up to your torso (similar to curling up into a ball) because it will make you seem defensive.

d. How to Look at People like an Alpha Male

We've all heard the saying that the eyes the windows to your our souls. So, show people your soul while looking into theirs, the power of your look is a very strong tool. This is how you do it.

Look Directly Into People's Eyes

It's quite intense looking someone in the eye, it shows that you are very engaged with each other even if you hold the stare for only a second longer than usual. Look at everyone when you enter a room and when you are having a 1 on 1 conversation with someone (women especially) alternate from one eye to the other and then look at their mouth. It will put the image of you kissing her in her mind.

e. How to Behave Around Women like an Alpha Male

The way Alpha Males behave around women is really different, but in general, there are a few constant traits that every Alpha Male will share. I could write a whole book on this topic alone but here are the important tips:

1 - Do Not Care What Others Think About You:

An Alpha Male has high self-esteem. He will behave however he wants without being fazed by the opinions of others. He will express his opinions, beliefs and desires as honestly as possible. Beautiful woman intimidates Beta Males but an Alpha Male will never feel overwhelmed or believe that he cannot be with that woman because he is not good enough. He wants her but does not need her.

2 - Never Cross the Line:

Its varies from culture to culture but in general playing touching and hugs are fine, but grabbing her ass anywhere apart from within the bedroom is way over the line and unacceptable.

3 - Be a Little Naughty and Playful:

In other words flirt. An Alpha Male will enjoy the company of beautiful women and will let his inner true-self free. This means sitting next to a girl talking about the weather when you honestly want to say she looks beautiful and amazing in her sexy dress is NOT being honest, and women will pick up on this.

4 - Become Well Cultured and be a Gentleman:

Women love a man with good manners and a great head on his shoulders. Watch some of the top 100 movies of all time and see which ones you like and do not like, then develop a small opinion on them. Read the top 100 books ever written because there is a reason they are read by so many people, so find out why and develop and opinion on them as well. Women LOVE a man who knows what he enjoys and does not enjoy, but even more, a man who knows why.

5 - Talk to A LOT of Women:

This is not as much of a trait but a practice. By talking to so many different types of women (Women you find beautiful, young, old, interesting, boring, etc..)

you will become comfortable around them and realize that women and just like any other human being out there. Just keep in mind that you are a confident Alpha Male. Show them all that you feel great in your own skin.

CHAPTER 7: GROOM AND DRESS LIKE AN ALPHA MALE

Society nowadays makes it very difficult for women when it comes to looking beautiful. There is a reason why women take much longer than men when it comes to getting ready for a date or anything in general. Women have SO MANY things to worry about when it comes to their looks. They have to take care of their hair, make-up, matching clothes, their shoes, their lingerie and all the different types of outfits available for them. And take note how I did not mention lady grooming, which is a whole other word altogether.

Now, men have it easy. There is not much for them to worry about, which is kind of great for us!

There isn't much pressure on men in terms of their looks and appearance, which means that with just a little effort you can start looking really good and probably, be the only one around that looks as good since most men do not tend to care much about their grooming and dress.

Alpha Males meet beautiful women everywhere they go and with this in mind they will be presenting the best of themselves. Let us begin with how to dress like an Alpha Male.

a. Your Clothes Must Fit!

Many men who are insecure about their bodies will use larger fitting clothes to hide their fat or clothes that fit them too small attempting to look more muscular or lean. Both these options fail horribly and you will never be seen as an Alpha Male. You need clothes that fit and are proper to the body type you have. When done properly it will GREATLY increase how attractive a man you'll be. Here are a few tips for different articles of clothing an Alpha Male can use.

1 - Jeans:

Finding a pair of jeans that fit can be a very long and tedious journey for some men. It really comes down to your body type and personal preference because every Alpha Male has a different style than the next.

Some prefer that their jeans relax comfortably off their waist while others can rock the skinny jean look. One indicator is using a few notches on your belt, which is a complete necessity for any man, so for beginners start with a nice black and brown leather belt.

The length of your jeans is also an important idea to focus on. They should sit easily on the top of your shoes with only a slight break at the bottom. One trick is to find a pair of jeans that reach right above your heel when you try them on without your shoes on, so that when you shoes are on they will cover your sock without sagging.

2 - T-Shirts:

T-shirts and jeans have been a great combination since the times of James Dean and Elvis that are used by Alphas all around the world. It's a classic and simple look that when paired correctly can really help a man's appearance.

In order for this to work, you need to have a t-shirt that fits. The shoulder seam should end at the END of your shoulder, any less and it will look too tight and any longer will make the t-shirt sag. The sleeve should end around the middle of your bicep but this is not as important since different styles are also popular. What stays consistent is the shoulder length and this will give you a nice broad look, a characteristic many Alpha Males shares.

I understand that many men workouts and it is very tempting to show off your guns by wearing a shirt that will be too tight to further emphasize their lean bodies. DO NOT fall for this trap! You will look silly and you will be made fun of. It may not seem funny at first but they do have a point. You look funny.

Now with the fitting out of the way, I can say that when it comes to t-shirts, it's really all about personal preference. Variety is a good place to start until you find what really works for you so buy a few rock t-shirts, some cotton V-necks that are very popular now or just a t-shirt from your university or city. T-shirts are very good at giving off a relaxed and confident look that will make women feel relaxed and confident around you.

3 - Dress Shirts

This one is very important as this what you will probably be wearing when you are out on a date or in the bar seducing the ladies. There will be many occasions where a dress shirt will be needed and finding the perfect one will make these occasions much more enjoyable. A dress shirt that is too tight will make you look ridiculous and a man who wears a dress shirt that is too large will be struggling to keep the thing together all night.

Sleeves are another issue that men have with regards to the fact that they did not fold them correctly, are too long or the sleeves are too short. If you are going to fold them then 2 - 3 folds will do just fine. The most important tip would be to find yourself a good tailor and invest in him to make you look good because it will pay off like you cannot imagine in the long run.

4 - Suits:

Suits are an iconic symbol of the Alpha Male attire. Some men wear them much more often than others but in general, a man looks confident, sharp and very handsome in a well-tailored suit. With that being said, all men should own a good suit. All Alpha Males need a suit. You will notice how confident you fell and so will women around you. So here's how to get it right.

Your jacket should hug your shoulders nicely, slim around the body and cover your bottom. As for the pants, they should be slim and not skinny and a break that will slight show   your sock when you sit down. It's nearly impossible to get all this right when you buy the suit at first; so going to a tailor is a must.

For those who do not own a suit you should aim to get one that to gray or navy blue, these colors will are overall accepted in any scenario either is be in the office or the bars.

A black suit might sound appealing but they only are used for night events, although they make you look for modern and stylish. You can pair your suit with simple t-shirts and Derby shoes to give you a different style when you are out, but all really depends on your preference. Just remember that the area of highest importance to making sure it fits well.

5 - Shoes:

Many men have problems what shoes to buy by not knowing what would look good on them and what will not, or they are not aware of what shoes they need to what occasions. Before any major tip, you need to make sure your shoes fit. If they are too big then walking with confidence will be difficult with your foot sliding all around your shoe. While shoes that are too small will cause discomfort all day and night.

Apart from fitting well, the most important tip would be: know what shoes to wear during different events. It's extremely tacky and unattractive seeing a man wear white sneakers at an event where formal shoes are the norm. I'm not saying you cannot experiment and find a unique style with your Nikes and suit, just make you are aware of the fashion norms women are very attracted to.

Every man should have a pair of black shoes and brown shoes for their formal events and the only think you have to worry about is matching it with your belt that is also highly recommended for men to wear. As far as sneakers go, since there is such a large variety of designs and styles, the only thing that remains constant is the colors used. So either you are you a sneaker head or a Vans fan, matching the colors of your sneakers to you tops will be great on the eyes when women notice your nice style.

Last important point is to keep your shoes clean and well maintained. It's quite simple, just dust them and brush them if you have sneakers and shoe shine on your formal shoes. For many women the first thing they notice from a man is his shoes, most women love shoes so they are very keen on them.

b. Find Your Style

Before we move onto grooming, I have to touch the topic of *Finding Your Own Style*. What I mean to say is you need to find a certain style that fits the way you are. You need to dedicate time and thought into what your style will say and what it says about you. Alpha Males indeed dress to impress but they all their own way of expressing themselves.

I used to know a guy who would dress very "preppy" and it fit his personality very well, he felt comfortable in his own clothes and skin. Then one day, he met a very beautiful woman who has a very gothic influenced style, in his attempt to seduce her, he started dressing similar to her.

Immediately we started to notice he was not very comfortable with his attire and he started to seem "out of place." Now the reason behind his problem was this style did not fit his personality or who he was at all. Clearly the lady could see right through his games and mentioned that when they first met, my friend would dress very conservatively and when she saw him again he looked completely different.

He admitted that he dressed that way to impress her and that brought out a good laugh for the woman. She also said that it was his initial preppy style that caught her attention because he looked so confident and comfortable when dressed that way. After this little conversation they had, my friend went back to his normal style and they both started dating feeling comfortable with each other's styles. Moral here is to stay honest to yourself and dress how you want to dress. You do not need to change your style to impress women because just seeing you comfortable in your own skin is enough to impress them. Just do not forget the fundamentals I originally taught you.

c. Grooming

Grooming is an essential factor in the life of an Alpha Male. Not only because you will look clean and good but because it shows you respect yourself enough to not look bad. If you look bad, you will feel bad and soon enough bad things in your life will start to happen. You will start to gain respect from those around when you begin to respect yourself.

Whether you cannot stand to look at yourself in the mirror or you just want to improve a little your appearance, these grooming tips will immediately make you look better and help bring out your inner Alpha Male. When women start noticing how good and clean you look, your confidence will multiply.

1 - Close Shave:

A big woman repellant is having untidy facial hair and a beard that is all over the place, even more if you happen to find food in your beard. You have two options: which is to either give yourself a clean shave with a proper razor blade to show off your smooth skin or you can trim/style your facial hair. If you go for the latter, I highly recommend going to a barber first to get an idea of what kind of facial hairstyle fits you.
This alone will make you look very attractive immediately. Taking with you confidence and pride everywhere you go.

2 - Take Care of Your Skin:

Many men believe that just splashing water on their skin is enough for it to be clean, which will then lead to dry skin with some acne on the side. It's worth it to invest in a facial grooming kit. Make sure you have a facial cleanser and moisturizer (even better with sunscreen.) Do not mistake taking care of your skin as a feminine activity. Taking care of your skin will go a very long way with the ladies. Simply wash your face in the morning with the cleanser then apply moisturizer and repeat the same at night before you go to bed.

3 - Get a Good Haircut:

Many men do not take proper care of their hair or even care what it looks like at all. They will simply get up in the morning, give it a few touches and leave the house looking horrible and untidy. Remember, not taking the time to respect how you look will cause others to lose respect for you as well and MANY men are like this. Separate yourself from the pack, be unique and get yourself a decent haircut.

Cut it to a short and easy to manage level, cover any gray hairs and if you are balding then just shave it all off, there is nothing worse than a comb over. Something simple such as asking for a #1 on the sides and a little longer on the top will make any man look cleaner and in general frame their face well. Your hair should be a high priority when it comes to grooming due to its major impact on your appearance and confidence.

4 - Clean your Nails:

Now this one is a little underrated but women have a particular eye for a man's nails. This includes having dirty nails and nail biting, which makes your nails crooked and in many cases red and sore. A man with poor nail hygiene will be doubted by many women and people in general because they did not pay attention to the fine details. Therefore in a way, no matter how much you put into your outfit and look that night, if your nails are disgusting then everything will be canceled out and you will just be another guy who doesn't care about his appearance.

A manicure and pedicure go a very long way and it's quite relaxing once you let go of the feminine aspect of it, similar to a massage. Although underrated, this one should as well be high on your Alpha Male grooming priority list.

5 - Live Healthy:

Not so much for the aesthetics, but more for the overall good feeling you are going to have and the surplus of energy you probably don't know you have. A balanced diet it a good way to stay healthy but if it's an issue getting different kinds of foods, then purchasing a multivitamin will do the job as well.

Working out regularly is also a great way to "groom" yourself. The gym is a great way to relieve stress and when someone is stress-free always seem to look younger, brighter and overall happier. If the gym is not your thing then any physical activity will do you wonders.

Stop smoking and limiting how much your drink is also a good way of staying healthy, smokers tend to look older and have bad skin as well as make your teeth look horrible. Initially, you will have a good high but in the long run, you will not live very long.

Any of you guys who aspire to be Alpha Males I urge you to please follow these tips. Make them into a habit and you will see a big change in your life, the way you are treated and the way women will see you.

I understand it's difficult but through discipline and slowly changing your body for the better good you will gain the confidence to achieve whatever you want in life. Take these tips, apply them to your life and your confidence will grow as well at the different opportunities that will appear before you. Just be the Alpha Male and do it.

CHAPTER 8: ALPHA MALE AFFIRMATIONS

An Alpha Male knows he is the man, he knows he is the leader, and he needs no one to tell him that that because he will constantly tell himself. These are Affirmations an Alpha Male will give himself to assure that he gets his daily pep talk. As previously stated, we all have the potential to become Alpha Males; all we have to do put in is the work.

You need to tell yourself you are the man because it is your own opinion that matters. You may receive these compliments from others but it will be in terms of their standards. Although compliments are meant well, the only standards that should matter to you are your own.

Self-affirmations are positive and encouraging statements that will help give yourself a good perception of yourself. They will help change negative behaviors, achieve your goals and repair any damage caused by negative affirmations.

How many times have you heard a friend or even yourself say, "I'm not good enough for this girl" or "I'm too fat or poor or ugly or unpopular"? These are all negative self-affirmations that we repeatedly tell ourselves that actually lead to negative behaviors that will make us act just like the things we are saying to ourselves.

An Alpha Male will never say anything negative to himself. To an Alpha Male, the only words about him that are true are the words that come from himself, which is why it is so important to make the words as positive as possible. Now, these affirmations are very easy to make but you need put yourself in the right mindset when you say them to yourself and well as have the motivation to truly believe what you are saying to yourself. Let's begin with how you to start your affirmations.

- **Sit down in a place where you can be alone, self-affirmations should be done between you and yourself, no one else should be involved.** After you have found a comfortable spot, start by trying to decide what you want. Is it to quit smoking? Be less afraid? Be an Alpha Male? Whatever is it, write it down and keep the idea in your head.

- **The very first thing we need to do is to focus on our positive attributes.** Many people rarely focus on attributes that they like about themselves but spend more time on things they want to change about themselves, which is a common form of negative self-affirmation. Make an inventory of your best qualities and abilities, either it is you being handsome or a responsible student/employee, make sure to write it down. After you have an idea, write down a short sentence that says, "I am handsome" or whatever it was you wrote. Use these are positive self-affirmations for yourself.

a. Positive Affirmation

We just went over the concept of self-affirmations, what they can do for a man and how to exactly make them. Now, having positive affirmations are perfectly fine but we also previously stated that through affirmations we could change behaviors. With that said, I will now teach you what an Alpha Male will say to himself and how he utilizes what he says to get what he wants.

First, write down a list of goals or a list of any negative behaviors you have. The list of goals is a list that requires certain behaviors that we currently do not have, and we will use Alpha Male affirmations to behave in a way that will allow achieving our goals.

When it comes to the list of negative behaviors, these are beliefs about ourselves that we do not like and we will use affirmations to change them. Self-affirmation is a tool that can be used in many different ways.

Before we start on the list, I want to give you some self-affirmations that an Alpha Male will tell himself to be the man he is. Here's a list of things you should write down and say to yourself. There are three types of positive Alpha Male affirmations:

1 - Present Tense:

These are affirmations that state what you currently are.

- I am an Alpha Male.

- I am dominant.

- I am always relaxed and calm.

- I am assertive and powerful.

- Others see me as powerful and self-assured.

- My confidence is solid and sure.

- All women are attracted to me.

- I can always take the lead in any situation.

- I am completely secure in myself.

- I speak with authority.

- I am fearless.

- People respect me.

2 - Future Tense:

Write these down if you are currently trying to become a certain way Alpha Males are but you just are not there. There is nothing wrong if some behaviors take longer to manifest than other, like I said, it will take time and dedication:

- I will become an Alpha Male.

- I am becoming more and more Alpha Male every day.

- I am finding it easier to take the lead in social situations

- My inner core self is slowly becoming more confident and assertive.

- Others are starting to notice my confident and self-assured attitude.

- People will respect me.

- I will always speak my mind.

- Women will be attracted to me.

- Women are starting to view me as a leader and as a confident man.

- I am becoming less afraid.

- I am slowly seeing an overall betterment in the way I am.

3 - Natural Affirmations:

These is similar to the present tense list but with the idea that these traits and behaviors and natural to us. We cannot change them and we accept them.

- I am naturally an Alpha Male and it is just the way I am.

- Women are naturally attracted to me.

- Confidence is my natural right.

- Being confident and assertive is just who I am.

- I take pleasure in being a leader in social situations.

- I enjoy being the Alpha Male.

- Others look up to my character.

- I make women feel safe and secure.

- I am highly respected.

- My Alpha Male traits allow women to feel more feminine.

- I am afraid of some things, but that will not stop be from achieving what I want in life.

These are the different kinds of affirmations an Alpha Male will say to himself to become what he wants. Now I want you to understand that every Alpha Males does NOT have every single trail or say all these things to themselves while sitting down legged crossed in front of a mirror every morning. They will choose one, and work on it, constantly repeating "I am fearless" when they are afraid or "I speak with authority" right before a big speech.

Let us now move into the how to attack our lists of goals and our list of negative attributes. How we will utilize our Alpha Male affirmations to achieve whatever we want. Again keep in mind, this is a slow life changing process where through dedication we really make a drastic change in our lives.

On many lists of a man's affirmations you will find "I am confident." or "I will be confident." This is a very broad statement that can apply to so many different types of situations. Let us set up the scenario of you in a bar and you see a beautiful woman. Right before you try to approach her, a giant wave of fear will consume your body and this is a moment you will need these affirmations you have said to yourself so many times.

"I am confident." Say it to yourself and believe it. Immediately you will feel less fearful and you will have to courage to speak to that women, and if you did not go, you have experienced the power of affirmation and next time you will feel even less fearful and it will encourage you to go talk to your future beautiful friend. Let me list down certain situations where different affirmations will help us prevail.

- You are about to enter a nightclub and you happen to see a man wearing a similar shirt to yours but more muscular when you compare your body types. Using the affirmation "I am an Alpha Male." will help you get over that insecurity. It is normal to experience these feelings, just know how to handle them and bring yourself back to the best person you can be.

- You are walking down a dark road with a date and it looks a little bit on the scary side, you notice your date is feeling afraid and uncomfortable. Here we could use our "I make women around me feel safe and secured" after we say this to ourselves and truly believe it then you will notice a change in your body language and boost in confidence. Your date will certainly notice as well which will lead to you to walking safely, her feeling safe and you looking like the Alpha Male in her eyes.

- You are currently at a business meeting where some of the people attending have more influence in the company that you do but you have a great idea that you would like to pitch to them. Our "People will respect me." affirmation will work great here but even before you pitch your idea, your body language and mannerisms will give off the Alpha Male vibe and the second you ask for their attention, you will have it immediately.

- You are dating a beautiful woman who went out with her friends and there happens to be a guy within that group who fancies your girlfriend. As a natural reaction, you experience jealousy and you begin to become paranoid and a little enraged at everything. A great affirmation here would be "It is completely normal to be jealous and have crazy thoughts. I trust and respect my girlfriend." Affirmations like these are crazy for calming the mind in a situation that just gives us the craziest thoughts.

- You are in an argument with a coworker and you guys going back forth over a certain action you believe the team should in order to succeed. Your coworker takes what you said, twists your words and makes them sound completely ridiculous when it was a pretty solid plan at to begin with. Here you may begin to feel that you are wrong and your coworker is right, a great affirmation here would be "I am not a crazy person. I believe in what I say and will stand by it until properly proven wrong." Once you have this mindset, your coworker will become intimidated and give in to your idea.

b. Negative Affirmations

Too many people focus too much on their negative affirmations without even realizing the damage they are doing to themselves. Unknowingly, they will believe that they will not get the job they are about to interview for, the girl who a guy is looking at will immediately reject him or a student having thoughts of failing his test right before he takes it.

By saying negative affirmations to yourself, you are putting your head in the mindset to act this way. What do you think will happen is you constantly utter to yourself "Oh my lord, this girl is not going to like me, she'll think I'm creepy if I go say 'Hi'?" She is probably not going to like you.

Even if said jokingly "Oh that was so stupid of me." will have a negative effect on you. I'm not saying that it's wrong to realize your mistakes but just do not go overboard. Please take note, some negative affirmations can be deep beliefs you have had since childhood, you may be surprised. Here's a small list of negative affirmations insecure people (we are all a little insecure) will say to themselves.

- I am not good enough.

- I am a bad person.

- That activity is too hard for me.

- I am too ugly for them to like me.

- I never win.

- No one likes me.

- I never have money.

- I'm sad.

This list is nothing compared to how many negative affirmations we will say to ourselves. Thankfully for the Alpha Male, these statements are easily counteracted with the proper positive affirmation. Let's take for example "I never win" this, at its very core, is a very hard negative affirmation to deal with. A person who says this to himself will ALWAYS feel like the "loser." No Alpha Male is a loser and by simply saying "I am not a loser" or "I always win" can be enough to overcome the negative affirmation.

Now for others, a simple sentence will not be enough to make you feel better again. Sometimes we need a proper elaborate positive affirmation, we could say "Losing is a part of life and in order to win I am going to have losses sometimes." As we stated before, becoming an Alpha Male through Alpha Male affirmations will take time and dedication. It will take a little while to believe in what you are saying, but never doubt yourself and you will be able to prevail over your negative affirmations.

Affirmations have the power to influence your behaviors, how you feel about yourself and how other will see you as well. This is why it is essential for an Alpha Male to have the most positive affirmations possible to ensure that he is getting his confidence and motivation from himself. A simple affirmation such as "I am a leader." will make you into the leader. Maybe not at first, but you will show very slight behaviors that will eventually become who you are.

More importantly, focus more on not using ANY negative affirmations at all. Oddly enough, a negative affirmation will influence a person more than a positive one. People, in general, are a little insecure and anything negative is more believable compared to a positive statement.

Eliminate all negative affirmations and when you say one to yourself then immediately counteract it with an Alpha Male affirmation.

Now men, focus on your own well-being and become the Alpha Male you deserve to be. It's all up to you my friends. If you believe you are an Alpha Male, then say it and affirm it.

CHAPTER 9: THE LAWS OF AN ALPHA MALE

We all have the potential to become an Alpha Male. Sadly, there are not many that actually push through. More and more weaker men are making an appearance who fear masculinity and who simply do not understand masculine values, which is the source of their fear. An Alpha Male is what society needs more than ever; there are too many weaker fearful men who are not ready for leadership roles.

By nature and history, men have always been leaders. Before we were the head of our families and tribes of whom we would protect, feed, and defend from any animals or attacking tribes.

An Alpha Male is a champion; a badass that does what he wants and society loves them. They do not fear confrontation nor will they run and hide. Alpha Males stand up and fight and it's these values that so many men nowadays are lacking.

14 Laws of an Alpha Male

Since I want you to be a man, a champion, and an Alpha Male. Here's a detailed list of values and beliefs that Alpha Males have at their core self, it makes them who they are.

1. An Alpha Male Must be Self-reliant.

Self-reliance is a dying virtue that will soon be gone unless the Alpha Males can reestablish the importance of it. There is a sense of entitlement being developed by many men who believe they deserve something when they have done nothing to earn it. Do not live sustained by others. Take care of yourself!

An Alpha Male must be as self-reliant as possible, everything in his life should be brought upon because he made it happen. His life, success, future and happiness must all be dependent on him. Only a weak man will let someone else dictate his life. If you can take care of yourself then you will be able to take care of everyone else.

2. Understand that Success and Happiness Require Hard work.

A common delusion is that success is something you are born into or randomly given to you and not something you work extremely hard for. Most billionaires are a self-made success. Also, the definition of success is not in terms of your career but a measurement of your happiness.

If you neglect the idea of success requiring hard work and that everyone has the potential be successful then you have lost. You will be a weakened man and life will end unhappy and unsatisfied.

3. Do Not Be the Coward Who Lives a Small Life.

Trial and error is an Alpha Male's best friend, it allows you try many different things and give you a broad selection of paths you can take and be the kind of man you want to be. The only problem is that you will fail, A LOT. Which will ironically be the cause of your success.

The only way to fail is to try something new and they only way to succeed is to keep trying after you have failed. You will have to face your greatest fears and defeat your demons in order to become the man you want to be.

4. Practice Self-denial.

Instant gratification is a characteristic of modern times. We are the generation of people who will purchase things we cannot afford to impress others. Many great men in history have shared the trait of self-denial. No work will get done and your dreams won't come true without it.

Just take it one day at a time. Find out what is hindering you in your life and remove them completely. It could either be TV, videos games or porn. Whatever it may be, remove it and replace the instant gratification with an activity that will help you move forward.

5. Always Stand for your Principles and Values.

There will come a time where you will be challenged and outnumbered.

You will have no one by your side but yourself and when this happens you must stand strong for what you believe in. When you find yourself on the side of the majority then maybe you are on the wrong side.

There's strength in numbers only because alone they are weak, but the Alpha Male is strong with someone or all by himself. Do not crave attention and acceptance from others. Society is heading in a direction where our values are directed more towards what people think of us. A real leader is unique, forms his thoughts and sticks to them.

6. Always Fight, Even When You Think You'll Lose.

Do not be afraid to get a little hurt, or living a hard life. The hardships are what make the Alpha Male so amazing and unique. Roosevelt was a fighter, as well and Bruce Lee and Napoleon. Also Mother Theresa and Gandhi who fought so hard and bravely for what they believed in, even if it wasn't through brute physical force.

Most men have never been in a real fight or struggle. If you have something to protect like your woman or your honor then do not be afraid to protect them. Same goes for your values, simply because they may not be popular does not mean they are not worth fighting for.

7. Do not be Afraid to Fail. Be afraid of not trying.

A coward will fear to fail and will never do anything. Many men are full of talk about their dreams and goals, but how many actually go and do it?

An Alpha Male says little and does a lot. His actions are what leave his mark, not his word. Even if his actions are a constant failure, he fights on until he finds success.

8. Be Kind but Not Weak.

Be kind and help others in any way you can, but do not be a doormat. Do not be kind because you think it is the right thing to do, but be kind because you feel this person deserves your kindness. Weakness is a lack of effort and caring for your ordinary man. Weakness is thinking of yourself.

Do not carry men but teach them how to carry themselves. Teach a man to be kind, not weak.

9. Be Just and Fair.

The idea of fairness has been destroyed with the upcoming of people who want what others have worked for without deserving it. Fairness is: You get what you deserve and earn.

As a man, you need to read this: A weak mentality is to envy what another man has or has accomplished, and think it not fair that you do not have the same. Fairness is not him giving you a little of what he has. Fairness is that fact that you have the opportunity to accomplish what he has accomplished. An Alpha Male will respect and admire the accomplishments of others.

10. Read Often and Read EVERYTHING

Read about your heroes and your favorite topics, but more importantly read about people and topics that completely go against your views. If you are an Atheist then read the Bible and if you are religious then read words published by Atheists.

Reading a lot has opened my eyes, changed my judgment and strengthened my character. I was able to leave my comfort zone just reading topics I did not agree with.

11. Unplug Weekly

Many people feel uncomfortable when in silence. We have been living a fast paced life that does not allow us to focus on a single idea but many ideas at once. Through this noisy life, we forget about our beliefs and values.

Silence is a valuable tool we can use to be grounded and remember what we truly believe in and reconnect with ourselves. Is it in silence where we find clarity, we will recharge and rediscover why are here and what is our purpose.

12. Do Not Live on the Internet

The rise of social media has been a large reason why people are spending hours online. Real interactions are becoming less common because men are creating a persona online of who they would rather live than their own lives. We never show who we truly are, only what we believe are the good parts of us.

An Alpha Male does not live on the Internet; he lives in the real physical world. Do not worry about your profile, how many likes you have or your online "friends."

Real friends are the ones who know you on a personal level. So, let the world see us for who we really are and not what is fake online.

13. Be Chivalrous

Chivalry is dying partly due to men not going the extra mile or because they were never taught how to be chivalrous when growing up. Another reason is it dying is due to the feminist movement and rising demand for gender equality.
As great as the movement is, it confuses men because instead of treating women as fairly as men, they will actually treat women like men. Most women want you to open the door for them, they want you to ask them out and they want you to take care of them.

Although not as popular as it once was, chivalry needs to exist. An Alpha Male understands this and lives by this code.

14. Be the Best at what you do.

It is NOT okay to merely exist and be average. An Alpha Male understand that he has to at least attempt to be the best in order to actually be the best at what he does.

If you are a father, you must be the best father for your kids, if you are a husband, then being the best husband is the only way. A fighter, be the best fighter. A man, be the best man. Do not accept mediocrity. Alpha Males always go beyond expectations.

Hopefully, this very brief set of laws will help you put on a path towards becoming an Alpha Male. You do not have to agree with all of them, which is ironically one of the laws previously stated, but make an attempt to understand everything you just read. Society is begging for Alpha Males, will you man up to the job?

Free Resources:

Facebook Page:
www.facebook.com/surefiresuccessnow

Website: www.workathomeentrepreneurblog.com

www.ingramcontent.com/pod-product-compliance
Lightning Source LLC
Chambersburg PA
CBHW060638290526
45793CB00001B/298

*9 7 8 1 5 3 5 3 3 7 7 6 2 *